PENCIL
techniques
graphite

Rahul Deshpande • Gopal Nandurkar

JYOTSNA PRAKASHAN

To Late Shri. Arun Phadnis, artist and art teacher, much loved by his students; and who always encouraged us wholeheartedly through all our artistic endeavours...

Publisher : Milind L. Paranjape,
Jyotsna Prakashan,
'Dhavalgiri', 430-31 Shaniwar Peth,
Pune 411 030

Mumbai Office : Mohan Building,
162 JSS Marg, Girgaum, Mumbai 400 004

© Rahul Deshpande and Gopal Nandurkar, 2012

Translation : Kalyani Nandurkar

First Edition : 2012

Reprint : 2013, 2015

Printer : Rich Print, 272 Narayan Peth,
Pune 411030

Price **SAKURA** Rs.600.00

ISBN 978-81-7925-277-2

Index

Introduction and History	5
Materials and Methods	7
Some Important Tips	19
Demonstrations 1 – 6	20
Gallery	32

Introduction and History

We find a pencil during our early days of childhood and instinctively start scribbling. With the discovery of this entirely new means of expression, begins a long lasting journey with the pencil.

Once this easily available and easy to use pencil and a piece of paper are found, it's the beginning of a creative journey. A pencil helps us give concrete visual form to things that we have seen and experienced, and things that we visualized in our minds. Practicing skills such as sketching, drawing and study sketches with a pencil are an integral part of art education. Professionals working with other allied branches of arts such as advertising, illustration, comics and animation art give expressions to their ideas with the help of a pencil. Same is the case with textile and fashion designing, architecture and interior and product design etc. The reason why such preliminary work is done using a pencil is simply because incorrect part can be corrected easily and in this way the entire drawing does not go waste.

Yet a pencil is not just limited to being an accessory for studies, it is also used to create complete works of fine art. A number of eminent artists with phenomenal mastery over pencil, pure sensitivity and genius have enriched the art history with their outstanding pencil works. The pencil that gives both line and tone is a source of countless creative possibilities. In this book, we have included techniques that contain various types of lines, combination of lines and tones, and drawing with tonal values only, for which different types of graphite pencil have been used. Other types of pencils such as Charcoal, Carbon, and Conté etc. will be described in the next book.

To review the history of the pencil, the word pencil is derived from the Latin word 'Pencillus' which means a little tail, synonymous with a small brush that was attached to the tip of a holder used by the Romans for writing purposes. Both Greeks and Romans knew that the metal Lead could be used to make a mark, and they used a thin disk made by Lead to draw guidelines for even lettering on the papyrus. Later in the 14th century, this disk was shaped into a rod and encased in a wood shaft. This became the world's first 'Lead' pencil, although it was very different than the actual lead pencil used today. The birth of the modern pencil can be traced to a storm in England in 1564, when a tree blew down and exposed natural graphite deposits or black carbon in pure, solid form. This substance was used to make black lines and marks. Since the chemistry of this substance was unknown at the time, it was named Plumbago meaning 'that which acts like Lead'. Later researches on Plumbago proved that this was a type of carbon that did not contain any Lead and was then named Graphite, which is derived from Greek word 'graph' which means 'to write'.

During the reign of Napoleon in early 19th century, both Germany and England had cut off all relations with France, cutting off Graphite supplies to France from these countries. During this time, a young French inventor Nicholas Jacques Conté developed an improved formula; in which he combined powdered graphite with clay and water, shaped into rods and were fired in a kiln. The resultant lead was durable and easy to use. This method also enabled control over softness and hardness of the lead by controlling proportions of graphite and clay. This method became popular and was adopted universally.

Leads of pencils available today are made in this manner, only they are now dipped into a wax solution, some of which seeps into the lead. Such wax-impregnated lead is smoother to write. The prepared leads are then encased in wood shafts.

There are two grades of pencils available, of which H grade stands for Hardness; the proportion of clay is more than graphite. Second grade B denotes Blackness containing more graphite than clay, hence is softer than H grade. In an HB pencil, both these properties are equally present. The degrees of hardness and blackness increase from H to 9H and B to 9B, respectively. Also, new forms of graphite pencils such as mechanical pencil, woodless graphite stick, water soluble graphite pencil etc. have been developed. Those types too have been included in this book.

We are confident that this book will encourage you to use a graphite pencil as a medium for creating art.

Materials and Methods

Pencils come in a wide variety of degrees of softness and hardness of graphite; 'H' denotes hardness while 'B' denotes blackness; 'F' is used to indicate fine point of the pencil.

Hard Pencil: As per increasing grade of hardness, these pencils available as H, 2H, 4H, 6H etc. are mainly preferred by architects, engineers and artists for clarity of lines got by these pencils. These pencils do not give darker tones, but are only useful for getting lighter drawings and tones.

Soft Pencil: Available in grades as HB, B, 2B, 4B, 6B, 8B according to darkness, these pencils are comparatively soft. By applying varying degrees of pressure, one can achieve tones ranging from light to very dark. Through this pencil, a number of drawing techniques expressing line and tone have been developed.

Mechanical Pencil: The leads of this pencil are available in a variety of thicknesses such as 0.3, 0.5, 0.7, 0.9 millimeters. By pressing the clutch on the back of pencil, the lead is propelled out. Main characteristic of mechanical pencil is that because of the lead size, the thickness of lines produced is always uniform. Also, since these pencils do no require sharpening, they are convenient for use by designers, artists and engineers.

Woodless Graphite: In this type, pencil leads (graphite sticks) are prepared without wooden or any other casing. A variety of these pencils is available according to the thickness and darkness of the graphite. For some types, a lead holder too is available.

Carpenter Pencil: Mostly used by carpenters, this pencil has a body with elliptical cross-section with flat lead. Specially designed for working on wooden surfaces, this pencil is flat and hard, and does not give darker tones.

Water Soluble Graphite Pencil: When a water-leaden brush is run over the rendering of this pencil, the tone is dispersed and turns into a watercolour wash. These pencils are available in a range of varying dark tones.

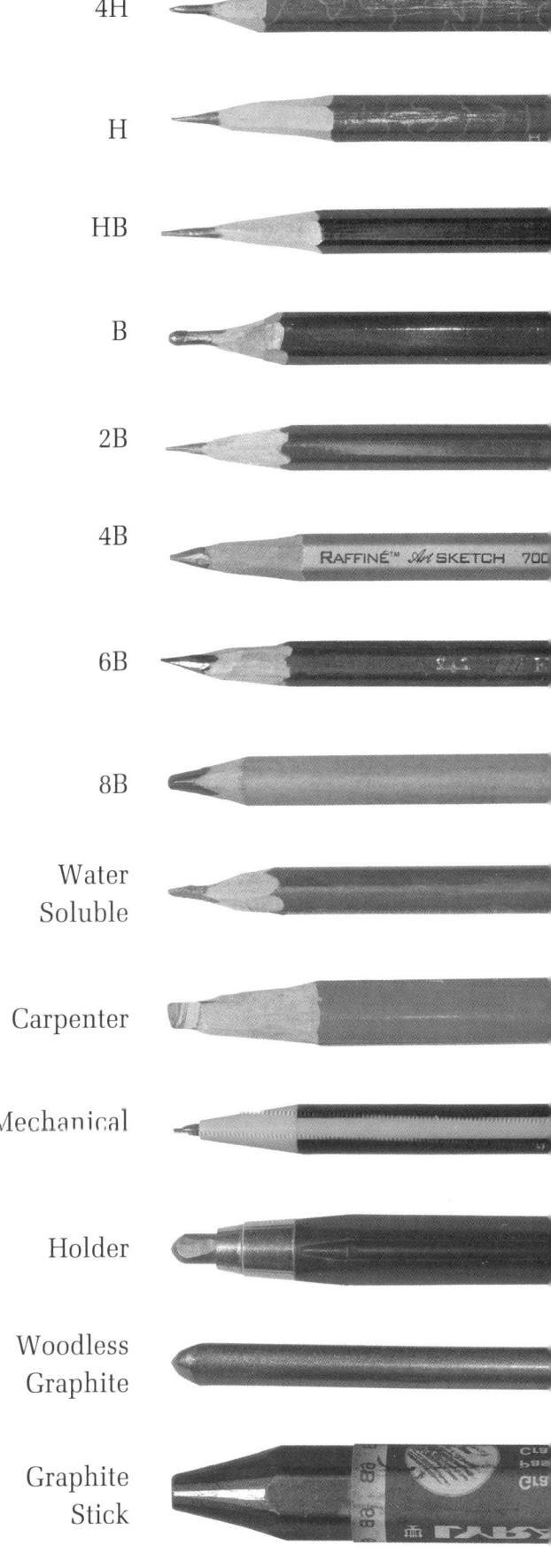

4H

H

HB

B

2B

4B

6B

8B

Water Soluble

Carpenter

Mechanical

Holder

Woodless Graphite

Graphite Stick

Different Types of Paper

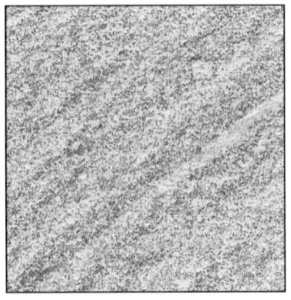
Cartridge Paper

Super white Drawing Paper

Lucky Parchment

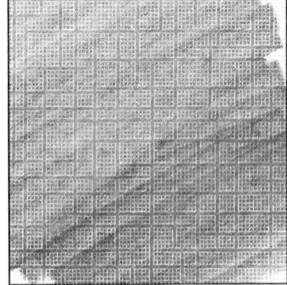
Mount Texture

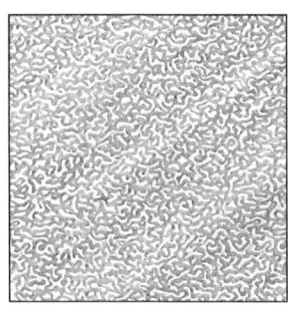
Leather Texture

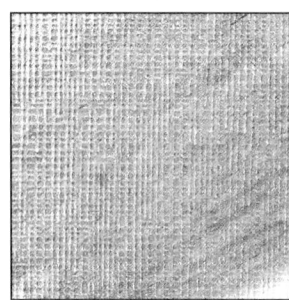
Linen Texture

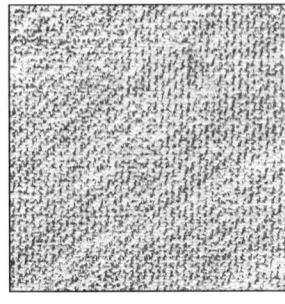
Matt-Textured Handmade

Medium-Textured Handmade

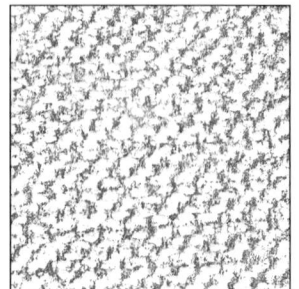
Rough-Textured Handmade

Along with pencil, selection of a paper is equally important. The effect of a pencil varies from paper to paper. Therefore, try to obtain different types of paper and experiment freely to understand how different textures can be achieved from each paper.

By mastering this aspect, one can easily select appropriate paper to draw depending on the subject, technique and type of pencil being used.

Other Materials

Eraser: An eraser is used to clean lines and marks produced by graphite pencils. Erasers are available in various sizes and shapes. When an eraser is rubbed on paper with pressure, it may damage the fibres on surface of paper and may even rip it; therefore it should be used delicately.

Kneaded Eraser or Putty Rubber: This rubber is made from pliable material that can be broken in pieces and shaped by hands to fine points which is useful for precision erasing and detailing work. Since no pressure is required to be applied, it is easy on the paper and does not leave any residue behind. This is now available in pencil form too.

Paper Stump: This is a stick made up of tightly wound paper with tapering points on both sides. The tapering sides are used to blend larger tones into each other and the points are used for detailing work. The paper stumps are available in assorted sizes. Similarly, finger tips are also used to blend tones.

Cutter, Knife, Sharpener: To sharpen pencil up to a desired point, a cutter or knife is used to whittle away the wood from its lead and then delicately shave the exposed lead to create as fine a point as is needed. Alternatively, inserting the pencil into a sharpener and twisting it delicately separates the wood shavings from lead and gives a fine point.

Sandpaper: Pencils which are soft are rubbed on a sandpaper to keep their points consistently sharp.

Fixative: Graphite particles when accidentally rubbed on other surfaces may smudge and spoil the drawing. To prevent this, fixative is sprayed over drawing. Fixative is actually a colourless varnish that forms a protective coating and is available in canned aerosol forms. When spraying, the can should be held about 15 inches away from the drawing.

Tracing and Butter Paper: Tracing paper is used to transfer pencil outline on another paper. Besides that, to prevent a drawing from smearing or spoiling, butter paper is used as a protective covering.

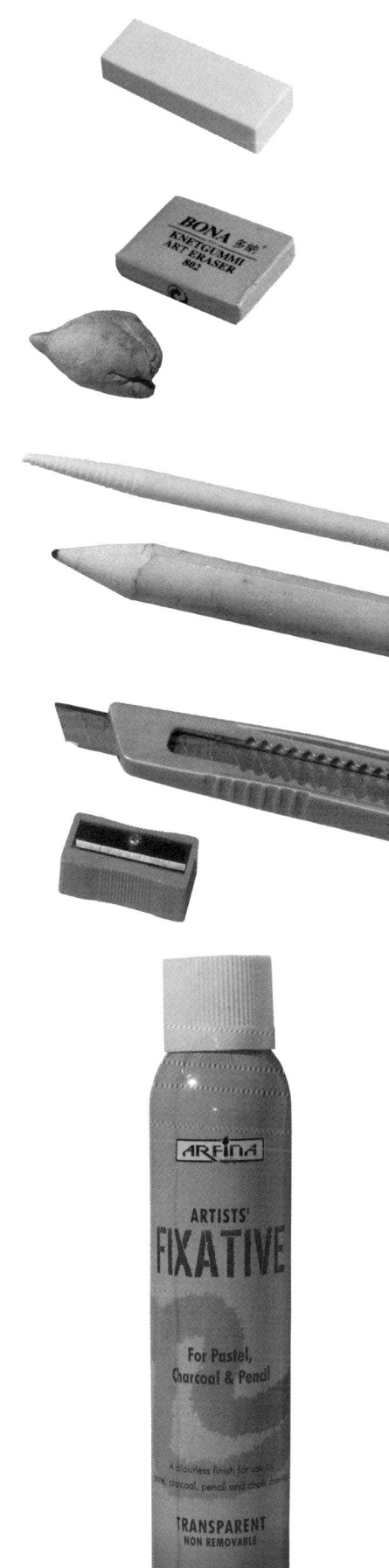

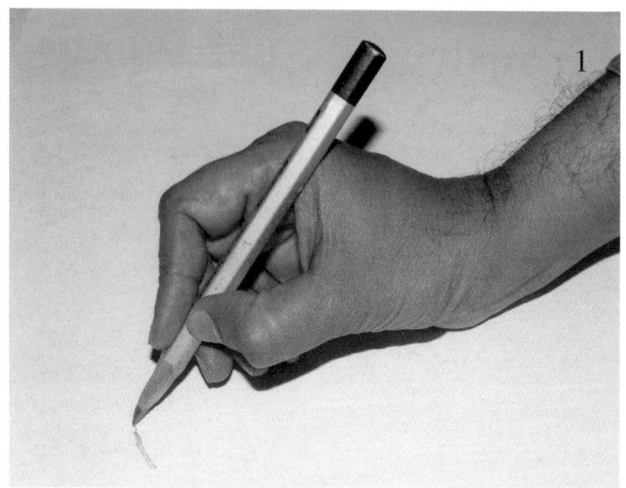
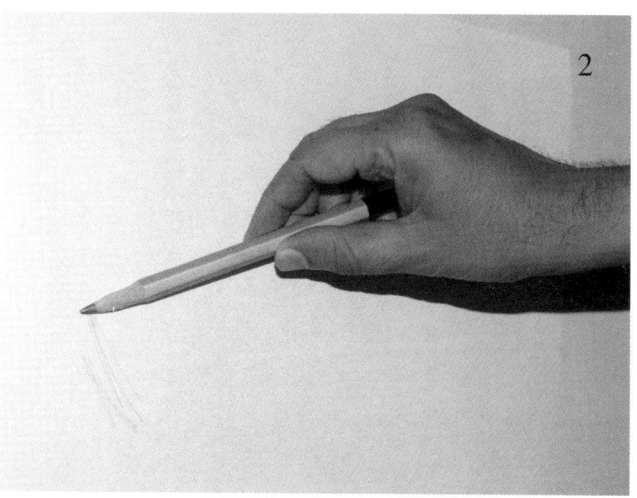
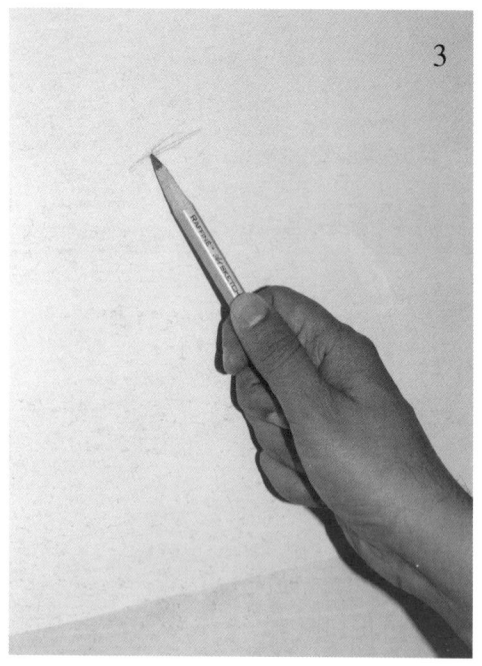

Types of Pencil Grips

1. Writing Style: In this style, the pencil is gripped between thumb and index finger with it resting on the middle finger firmly. Since the wrist rests on paper, there is some limitation to the movement of our hand. By holding pencil in this manner fine and short lines, filling even tones, working finer details are easily done.

2. Overhand Grip: Pencil is gripped by thumb and index finger but held under palm. There is no support of middle finger and the wrist does not rest on paper. This enables free movement of hand. This grip is best used to work on paper mounted on a slanted or vertical easel.

3. Pencil in Palm: Pencil is held vertically for drawing and hand can be freely moved from the shoulder joint. This helps work freely and used mainly for drawing on paper mounted on a vertical easel.

Even out rendering of tones with a paper stump

  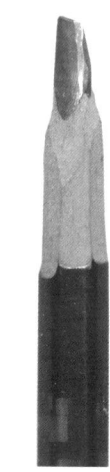

Fine Point   Blunt Point   Chisel Point

Types of Lines

Many types of lines can be obtained by a pencil point, but mainly there are two types, straight and curved. Drawing is developed with use of these lines. The lines can be used to achieve different types of textures. Such lines are helpful when doing sketches, drawings, studies and designs.

The lines expressed are sometimes rhythmic, forceful and delicate, the quality of each line changing as per the expression of the artist. Therefore a line gives a unique identity to an artist. An artist has to strive hard to achieve command over the line, after which he slowly realises the power of expressing more content in few lines. After achieving command over the line, expression comes with ease and it improves artistic quality; therefore ample practice of drawing lines is necessary.

Even Tones Horizontal Direction

Even Tones Slanting Direction

Even Tones Vertical Direction

Horizontal Direction Dark to Light

Slanting Direction Dark to Light

Vertical Direction Dark to Light

By using a pencil, along with lines we can obtain tones as well, which is its unique quality as a medium. While practicing to create tones using pencil, two major considerations are needed. Firstly to create even tones. Secondly, by increasing pressure on the pencil, gradually create light to dark tones. Here, it is shown how to create tones by changing the direction of pencil strokes.

There are countless hues and tones in the nature. It is impossible to express them as is while drawing. Therefore they are categorized into a gray scale with nine tones. According to this gray scale, simplify the tonal values of the view in front and then draw with a pencil.

Gray scale created using pencil tones

Light Tones   Middle Tones   Dark Tones

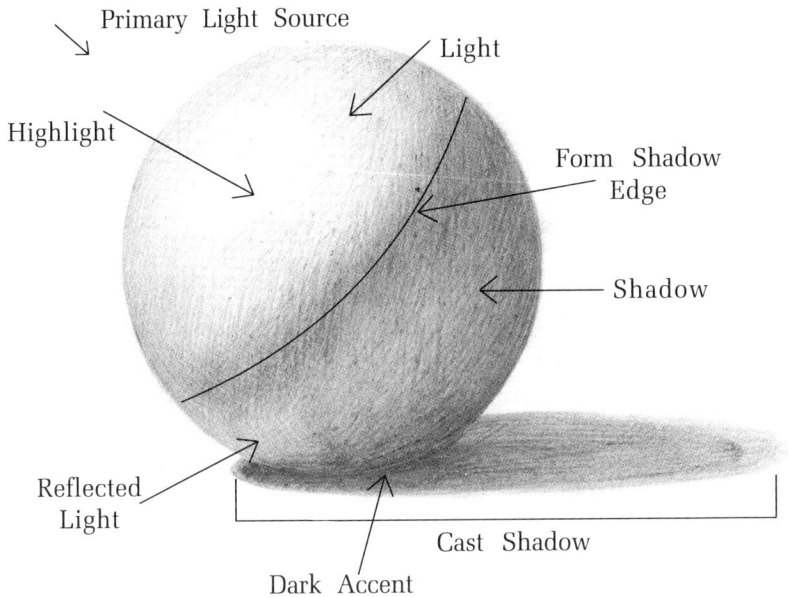

It is important to understand tones according to the shade-light effect on any object. These tones are divided into light tones, middle tones and dark tones according to the gray scale. The diagram of a spherical object on the left shows separation of light and shade on it and its relation with the tonal values.

Direction of light on the sphere is from top left, lighting up the left side and top of the sphere. This area is called the 'Light Portion'.

Opposite side where light does not reach is called the 'Shadow Portion'.

The place where shadow and light separates, a dark line is seen called as 'Form Shadow Edge.'

In the shadow portions, due to reflected light some areas are lit up where the tones are lighter, this is called 'Reflected Light'.

Shadows are created opposite to the direction of light. According to the direction and angle of the light, and its distance from the object, the shadows become longer or shorter. This shadow is called 'Cast Shadow'.

The part of the shadow nearest to the object is darkest in tone. Such parts are called 'Dark Accents'.

On the first sphere, direction of light is top and front. Due to this, the form of the sphere is not very clear and the shadow portion is almost negligible.

Light on second sphere is intense and from left side lighting up left portion and leaving right portion in the shadows. The shadow of the sphere too is very dark, leading to mixing of dark tones of sphere with its Cast Shadow.

On the third sphere, direction of light is from left with reflected light from right side decreasing the tonal values in shadow portion. Hence there is a clearly visible Form Shadow Edge at the separation of shade-light. The form and its Cast Shadow are distinctive because of the reflected light. Three-dimensional effect is more defined because of this type of light arrangement.

High Key

Middle Key

Low Key

High Key: When three tones of high value in the gray scale occupy more than 75% portion of the total, then the drawing is said to be High Key. For example, sky covered with white clouds, snow-covered lands, mist, rains, subjects awash with bright sunlight etc. are the subjects that come under this type. High key drawings generally look pleasant.

Middle Key: Like the name suggests, the three values in the middle of the gray scale form the Middle Key. Since the tones are close to each other, dark and light tones are used in these drawings to bring contrast to them. Colours are important in these types of drawings.

Low Key: Three tones on the darker side of gray scale primarily make up the low key drawings. Since these drawings comprise very dark colours, they effectively express evening, night, darkness, heavy shadows, mysterious atmosphere etc. Naturally, there is no room for colours here as the colours are blended into the values of tones themselves.

When starting to draw, it is essential to first understand the tonal values of the subject. This is important to bring harmony to the drawing. Accordingly, it helps us to select pencils for the work. For High Key, pencils in the grade of H, HB, and B are effective. Middle Key tones can be achieved with the help of 2B – 4B, and Low Key tones can be achieved by using 6B – 8B with varying pressures.

Line Approach

There are three basic methods of drawing; of which the first one is to draw using lines only. The external form of an object can be defined by means of lines. In this type of drawing approach, without considering shade-light effect, the search for beauty of forms and their relationship with each other is the main focus.

This drawing has been created using even rhythmic lines with slight decorative element added to it. For this mainly curved lines have been used. There are unlimited possibilities of expression using lines, but for which, constant attentive practice and consistency are needed.

Line and Tone Approach

In this method, tones are used along with lines. Tones are used to show the shade-light effect, structure of form and to create textures. Since in this method, lines and tones are the basic elements used, a wide variation in visual effects can be achieved. Therefore this method has vast scope for experimentation and creative possibilities.

This drawing was created by 2B pencil using only lines initially and then even tones were filled up as per shade-light effect. Lastly, tonal values were increased wherever necessary and dark tones to complete. Since there is a grouping of shadow portions, the subject is clearly expressed.

Tonal Approach

In this approach, line is almost negligible or completely absent. Various tones are grouped together to define forms in the subject. More importance is given to shade-light effect in this approach. Therefore hard and soft edges on forms are rendered to define an object. The tones formed due to intensity of light and their gradation is carefully rendered in this process. By using 4B, 6B etc. pencils, one can achieve a wide variety of tonal range in the drawing. It is important to minutely observe the changes in tones as a result of variation in planes of a form, and to note them down in the drawing. In this method there is effective portrayal of illusion of reality.

For this drawing, first a rough sketch was created with light hand. Then with 6B pencil, by applying varying pressure, tonal effects were achieved gradually completing the drawing. Lastly, dark tones were added wherever required.

Some Important Tips

- A range of papers are available from very thin newsprints to very thick handmade paper. These papers, depending upon their thickness and texture give a variety of rendering results. Therefore while choosing paper, consider the factors such as drawing technique and type of pencil that is going to be used.

- Texture of a paper is different on both sides; one side is smooth while the other is slightly rough. This difference can be discerned by feeling the paper with fingertips. The results of pencil shading are different on each side, so choose the side of paper accordingly.

- Due to the thickness of pencil strokes, there is a limitation on working large sizes, approximately 12 inches to 15 inches drawings can be worked effectively.

- Some drawing techniques are time consuming, requiring patience and consistency to bring it to perfection. At such times, enjoy the process of drawing and work slowly and steadily.

- Many times, undue pressure is applied on paper to achieve darker tones which may spoil the texture of the paper. It is better to switch to a darker pencil instead.

- Plenty of practice is needed to gain mastery over pencil medium without which work of quality cannot be produced. Therefore one should keep working constantly using pencil as a medium.

- While working with pencil, our hand may accidentally rub against the paper and may smudge the drawing. Therefore, it is better to start working from top moving down gradually and always keeping a piece of clean paper at the place your hand rests on the paper. Also try to keep the remaining areas of the paper clean and tidy.

- The pencil point keeps blunting and may produce variation in the thickness of lines as you work with it, therefore it needs to be sharpened from time to time.

- Due to the properties of graphite used in a pencil, we get a dark silvery grey tone instead of dark black tones that are obtained from charcoal and carbon pencils.

- Same subjects can be drawn using different methods and techniques as an experiment. This will help one understand various visual effects of different techniques.

- When working with pencil, first draw with light hands and then gradually increase tonal values. If necessary, draw correct and flawless outline on a separate paper and use tracing paper to transfer it for final drawing.

- To prevent finished rendering from getting smudged, always cover it with butter paper.

Demo 1 - Line Approach

Still Life, 2B

While defining outlines of the group of objects, their length and height were first marked on paper. Next, straight lines were used to develop the drawing by considering the placement of objects and their proportions with respect to each other.

After fixing the sizes, form of each object was observed and then drawn one by one. The structure of forms was precisely drawn using short lines.

For this drawing only lines were used, showing forms by forceful and free lines. Effect of light and dark lines has been obtained by applying varying degrees of pressure on pencil.

According to shade-light, highlights and light-shade division was depicted by lighter lines. In this manner, outline of the object, structure of form and division due to shade-light effect are shown using lines. In this method, there is emphasis on showing the three-dimensional effect of an object using only lines instead of tones.

Demo 2 – Line Approach

Landscape, Bold Lead Holder Pencil

A bold lead holder pencil is used for this drawing. Thick jerky lines were used to start drawing from one part of it. This process is called selective start. In this method, you can start drawing from any portion you want, completing that first and then moving on to other part accordingly.

Forms around the main portion were completed gradually. While drawing using lines, without considering shade-light effect, giving importance to only the composition formed by relationships between the forms.

Simplification of forms is presented avoiding details in them, and integration of bigger and smaller forms and linear tracks create movement in the composition. This gives a unique visual effect even without shade-light effect in the drawing.

Demo 3 - Line & Tone Approach

Landscape, 2B

The subject selected for drawing was first closely observed.

After observation, the important forms and their proportions with respect to each other were marked and general outline was drawn using lines.

Fine point of a 2B pencil was used to complete the outline by simplifying complex forms.

Hatching and Cross Hatching technique was used to render shade-light effects. Lines were used to achieve the effects of various tonal values which have given the drawing a unique visual quality.

Demo 4 – Line and Tone Approach

Portrait, 2B, 4B, 6B

Initially, linear structure drawing of the face was done by light hand. While fixing the outline according to these lines, the proportions and characteristics of his personality were closely observed.

Next, tones were gradually increased and shading was done according to the details of face and his turban and the shade-light effect on them.

All details and appropriate tonal values were gradually darkened completing the drawing. For his white beard, paper has been left blank in places. Rhythmic lines and lighter tones have been used to achieve this effect. Mixed effect of line and tone has been achieved in this drawing using 2B, 4B and 6B pencils.

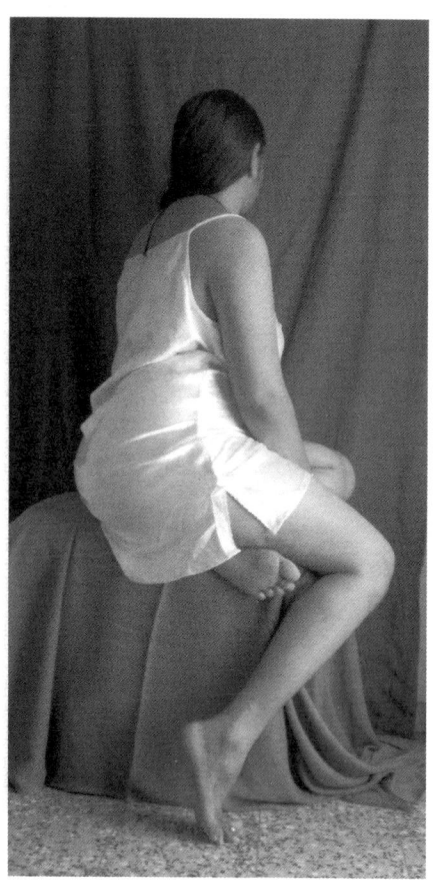

Demo 5 – Tonal Approach

Figure Study, 4B, 6B

While working from model, first structure drawing was done and then outline was developed with the help of these lines. All lines were drawn with very light hand and then started adding tones as per the shade-light.

Tones were used to achieve the effects of the structure of form, light portions, shadow portions, form shadow edge and reflected light, using hatching and cross hatching to do so.

Lastly, after deepening the tones around the model, the figure was highlighted. Deep tones and dark accents were used as required to complete the drawing. The 'moulding' of the figure is clearly defined due to hard and soft edges of the form.

Demo 6 – Tonal Approach

Portrait, 4B, 6B, 8B

This is an ideal subject for tonal drawing only. First, outline was fixed with light hand.

Then 4B pencil was used with light hand for tonal rendering. The method of deepening tones slowly and gradually was used.

A paper stump was used to achieve the smooth blending of tones, applying the pencil tones first and then rubbing paper stump on them to even them out.

First 4B, then 6B and for very dark tones 8B pencil was used. Lines are non-existent in this drawing. The form is defined using only tones and 'lost and found' edges express the three-dimensional effect well.

Gallery

▲ *Super White Cartridge – HB Pencil*

For this drawing, pointed HB pencil is used in 'Line and Tone' technique. Precise lines expressing the form and wherever necessary, limited tones have been used to complete the drawing.

◀ *Super White Cartridge – 0.5 Mechanical Pencil- 2B*

Lines formed by the mechanical pencil have a uniform thickness; hence it was used to get the texture of the leaves. For shadows of the trees, unidirectional lines are used to create a rhythm in the picture.

Alabaster Paper – 4B Pencil

The portions of light have been left white in both these drawings. Shadow grouping method is used for division of space between light and shade. This practice is useful to achieve simplification of forms in the subject and considering the picture as a whole.

Bond Paper – 0.5 Mechanical Pencil - HB Lead

This picture is created using only lines and without considering shade-light effects in the view. By doing this, it simplifies complex forms in the subject resulting in an integrated yet clear visual statement.

Super white Cartridge - 0.5 Mechanical Pencil - 2B Lead

In this technique, a 0.5 mechanical pencil that gives uniformly thick lines is used. The shadow portions are drawn using straight parallel lines with the help of a ruler. By varying the distance between lines tonal variation was achieved. Use of only vertical lines has helped enhance the magnificence of this architectural subject.

Super white Cartridge - 0.5 Mechanical Pencil - 2B Lead ▶

The use of 'jerky lines', short strokes and a little shading in some places has given this composition a unique visual effect. Without just producing a detailed portrayal of the objects in front, by similar selection and simplification process, we can search for new avenues.

Cartridge Paper – 6B

This is a tonal study. The texture and the shade-light effect of each object in this group have been expressed effectively using appropriate tones. A dark pencil like 6B is suitable for such drawings. We can similarly create different tonal studies by arranging things from our daily lives.

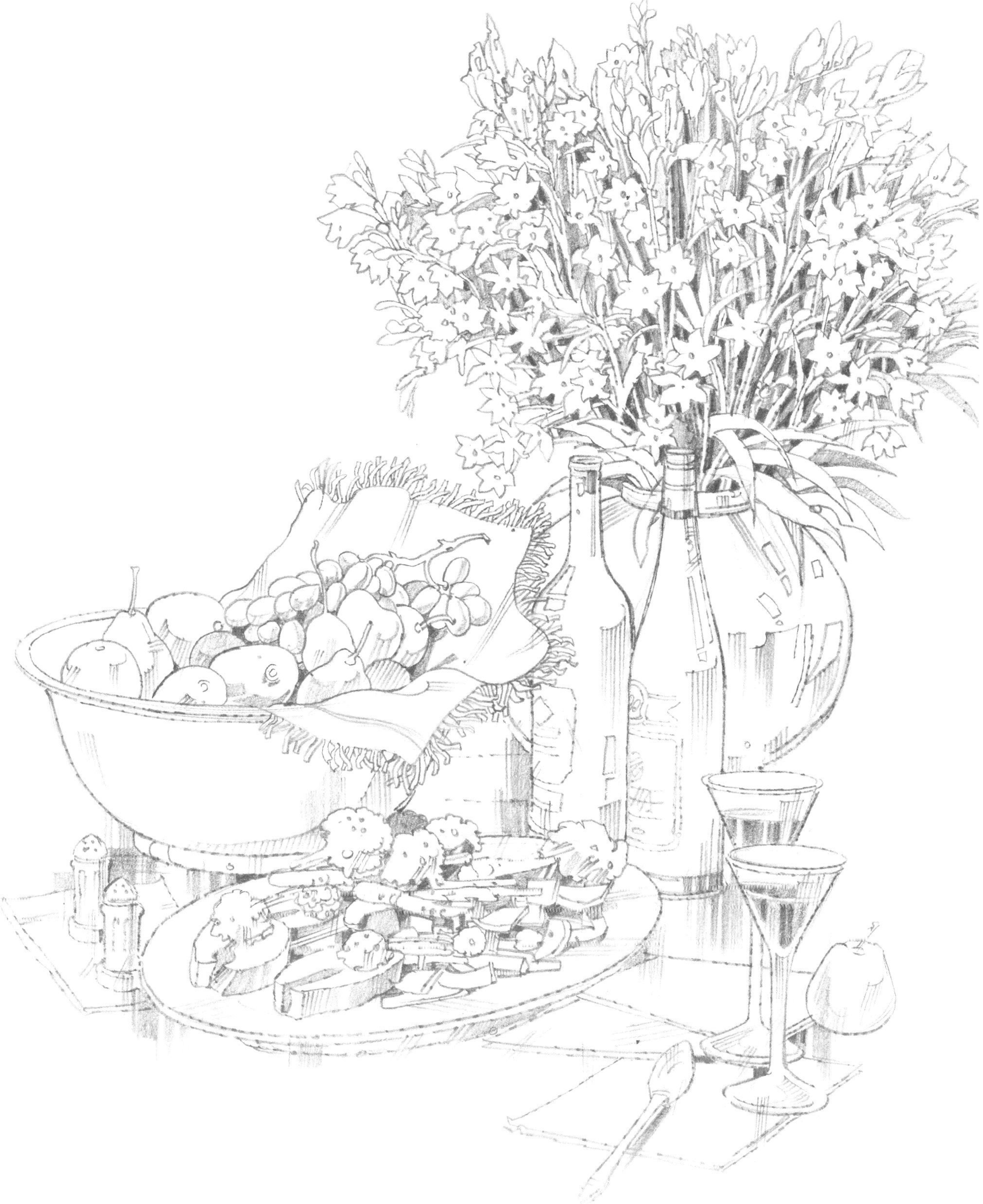

Super white Cartridge – B

Initial drawing was done using very light lines. Then, gradually increasing pressure on the pencil, tones were developed according to the shade-light and details added. Lastly, very dark tones were used to finish the drawing.

Natural Shade Cartridge – H, 2H

H grade pencil has been used to achieve the soft furry texture of this squirrel. Since this pencil is quite hard, it is easy to maintain the individuality of each short stroke. The lines were given directions according to the form.

43

Super White Cartridge – 2B, 4B

The soft glowing complexion of this young woman has been shown by leaving the paper white in the areas of light portion. The portions of shadow are shown by gentle strokes of pencil to get a smooth tone. Gently flowing lines depict the natural waves of her hair.

Drawing Paper – 2B

In the portrait of this old man, lines and wrinkles on his face are expressed using hatching and cross hatching technique.

It is obvious while looking at both these portraits that selection of the right technique according to subject helps make the drawings more effective.

Super White Cartridge – Graphite Stick

Initial structural drawing of this portrait was made using lines. Later the drawing was completed by gradually adding details and shade-light effect.

▲ *Super White Cartridge – Graphite Stick*

In the above portrait, forceful lines have been used to draw the face, hat and scarf according to the form and structure. Even though shade-light is not considered, the various planes formed by lines give it a feeling of three-dimensional structure.

Super White Cartridge - 0.5 Mechanical Pencil - 2B ▶

In this portrait, short parallel lines have been used with 'line and tone' technique to express dimensions and shade-light effect.

Drawing Paper – 2B

Figure drawing is one of the important subjects in the study of arts. A pencil that gives linear and tonal effect is useful for this subject. This drawing shows perfect proportion of a human form and shade-light effect on it.

Cartridge Paper – 4B

To express the dark and shiny skin of this young woman, smooth rendering of 4B pencil is used for light and dark tones.

Cartridge Paper – 4B

In both these drawings, three-dimensional subjects are converted into flat two-dimensional forms using lines. Limited even tones have been used to maintain the two-dimensional effect.

Drawing Paper – B

While portraying this young woman in traditional Japanese attire, her fragile beauty has been depicted with delicate rendering of pencil achieving a Sfumato effect. It is important to handle the pencil medium as per the subject demands for which one needs to keep experimenting constantly.

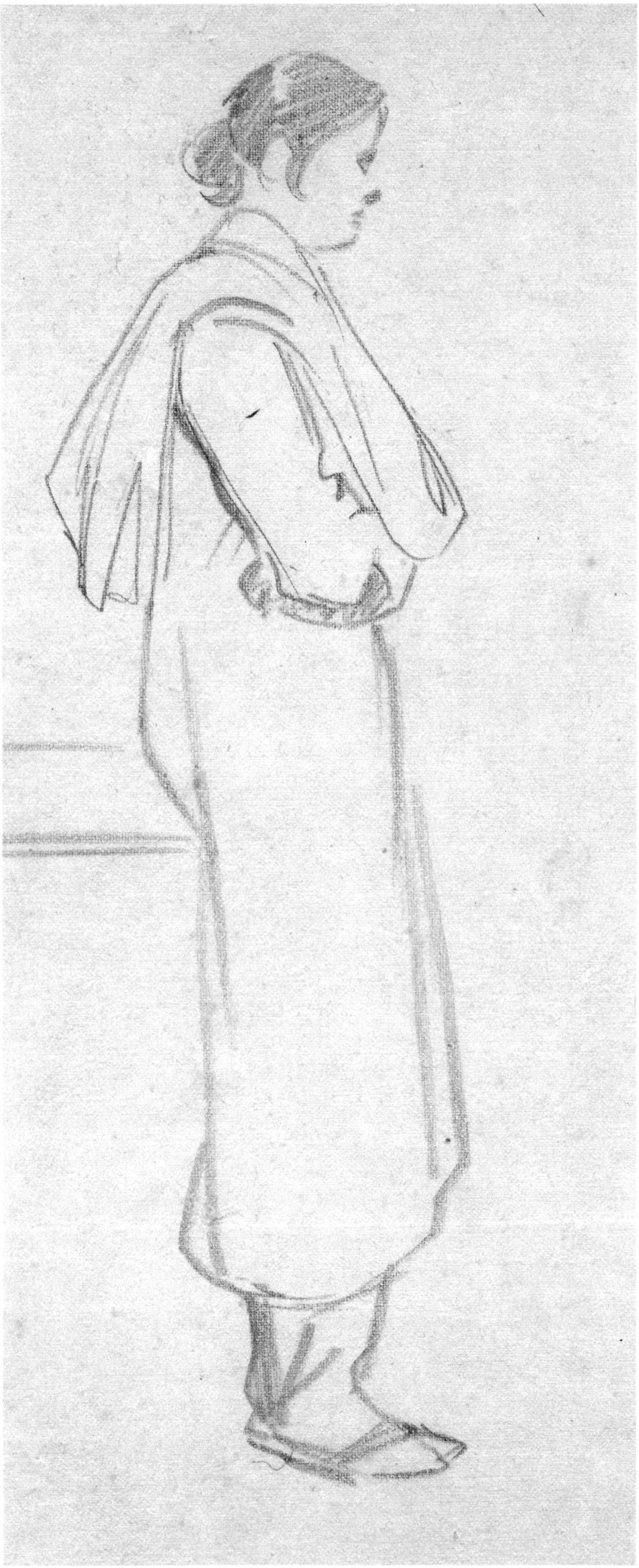

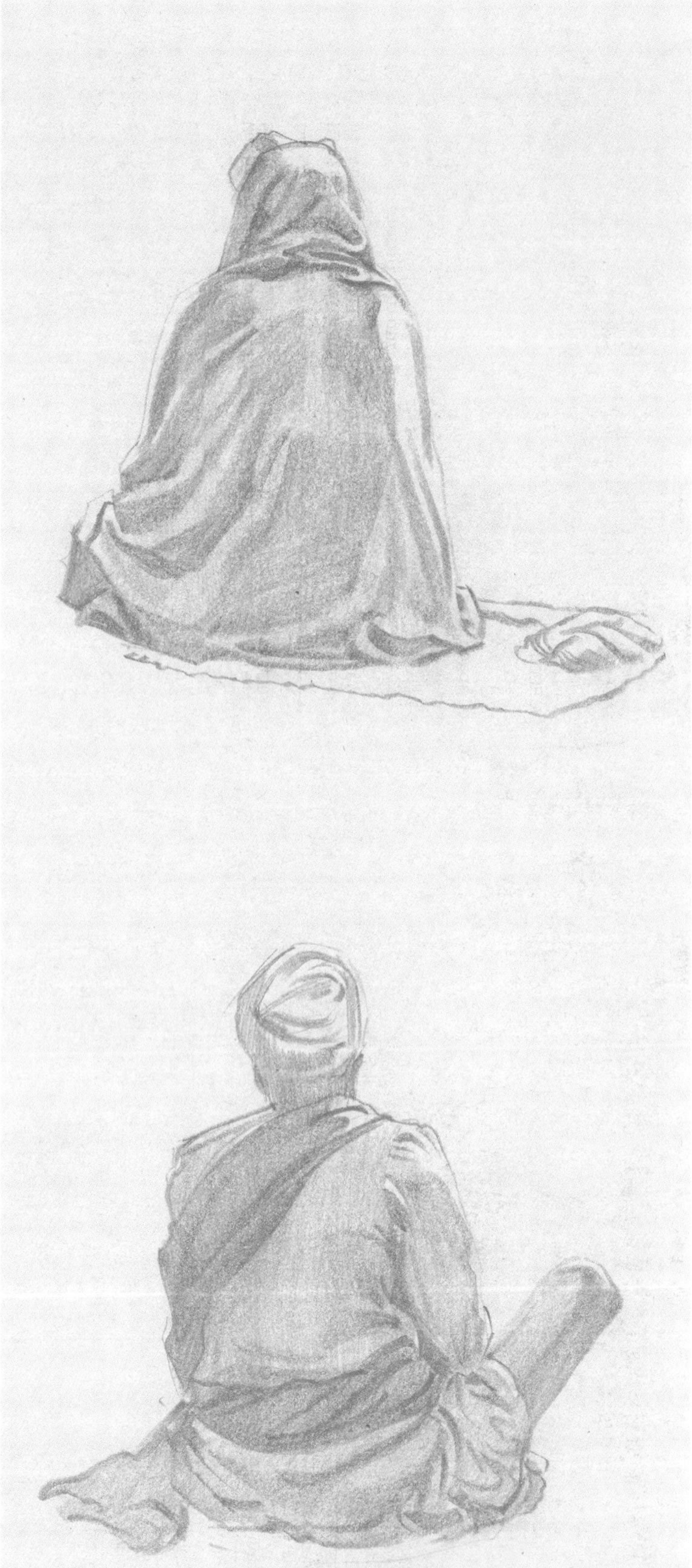

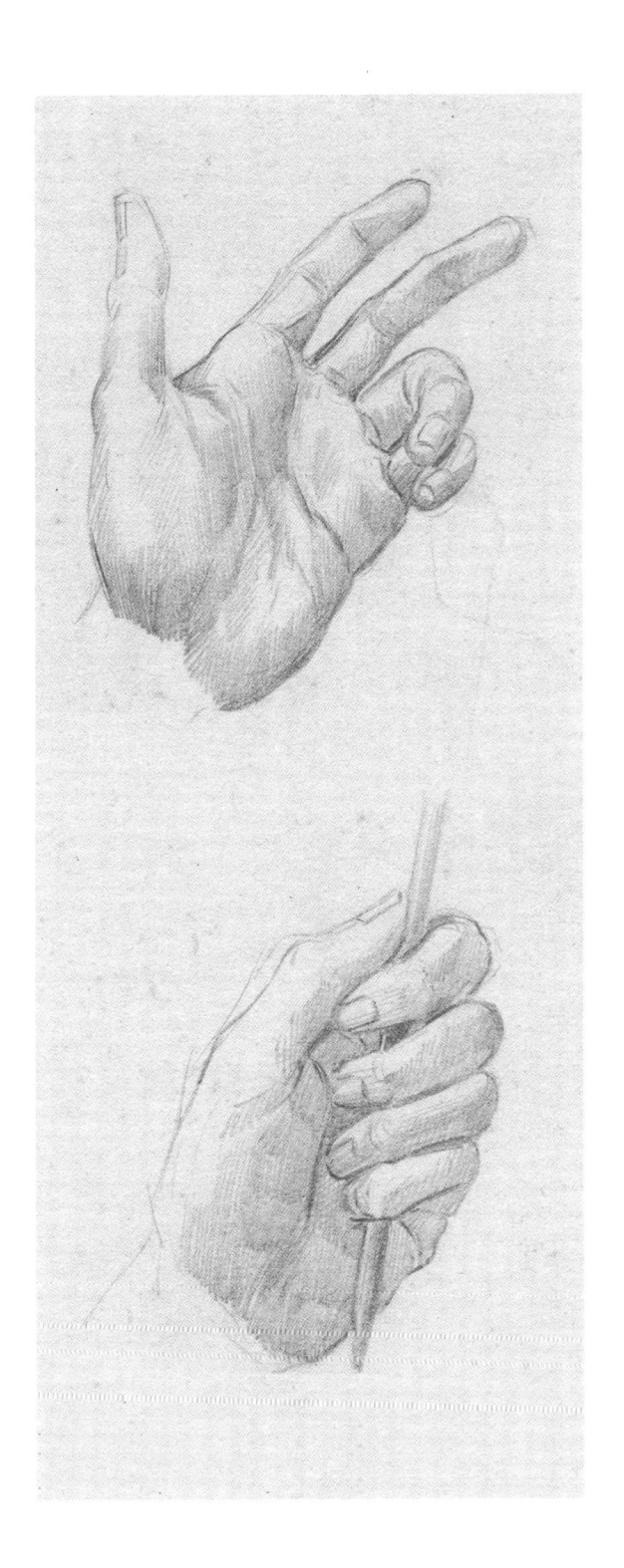

Newsprint – 6B

Some of the several benefits of sketching are, improvement of line and improvement in concentration. So one should practice it consistently. Along with it, drawings with study of shade-light also should be done regularly. Both of these are useful for memory drawing.

Bond Paper – 2B

Full forms of human figure are quickly rendered here with pencil. This type of studies helps to understand the figure as a whole. It enhances the awareness of proportions, actions and negative-positive forms. Therefore practice drawing with this approach.

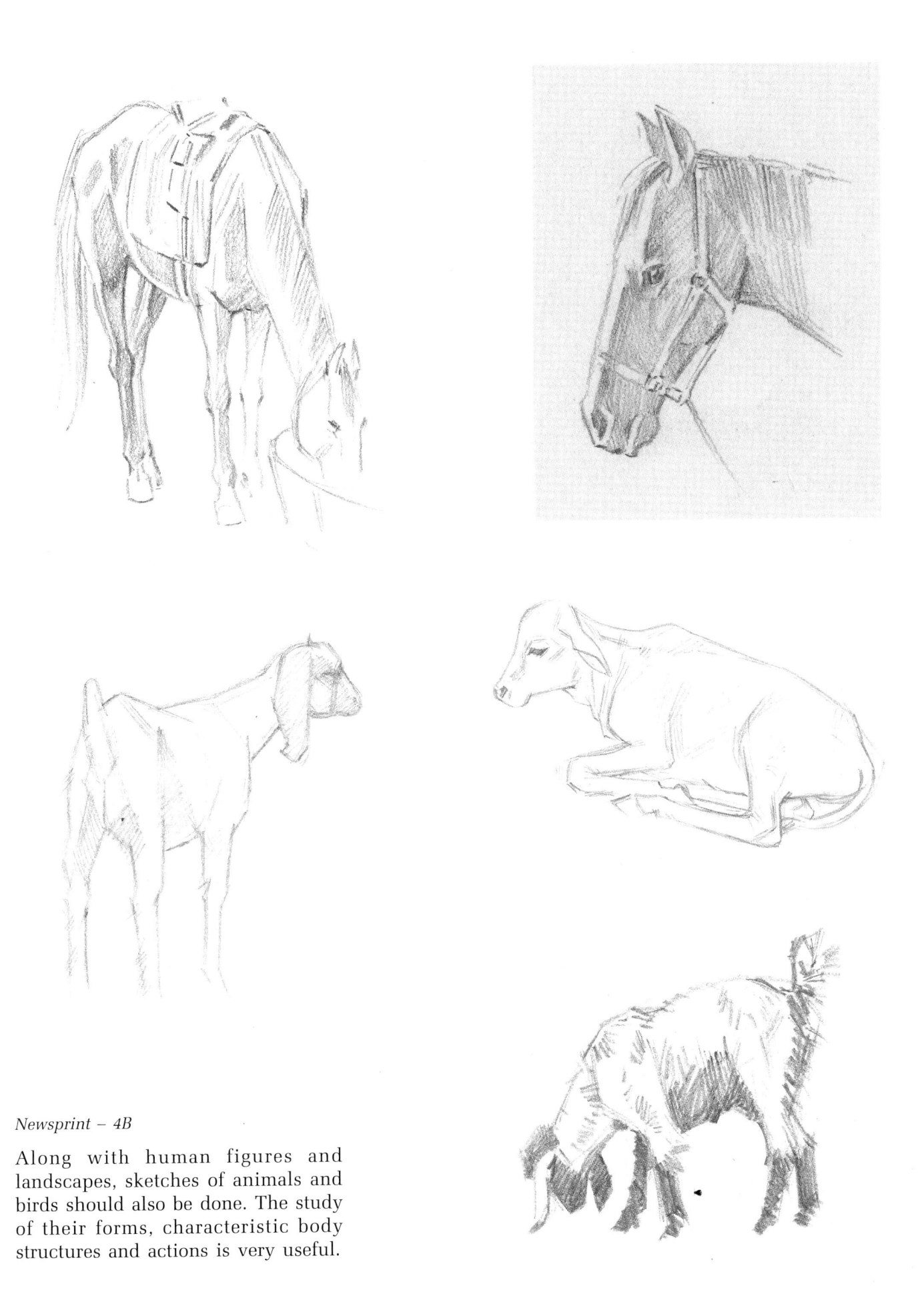

Newsprint – 4B

Along with human figures and landscapes, sketches of animals and birds should also be done. The study of their forms, characteristic body structures and actions is very useful.

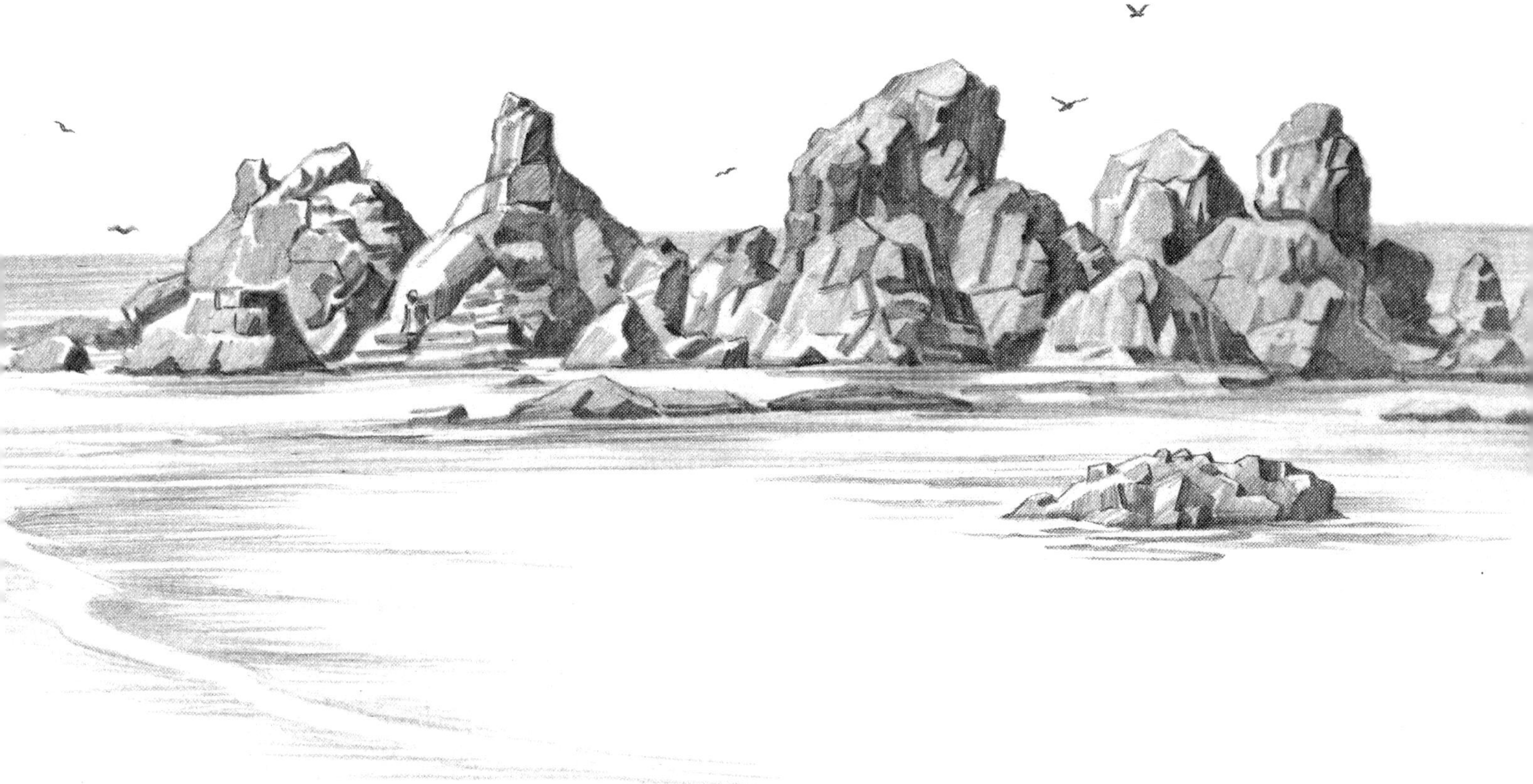

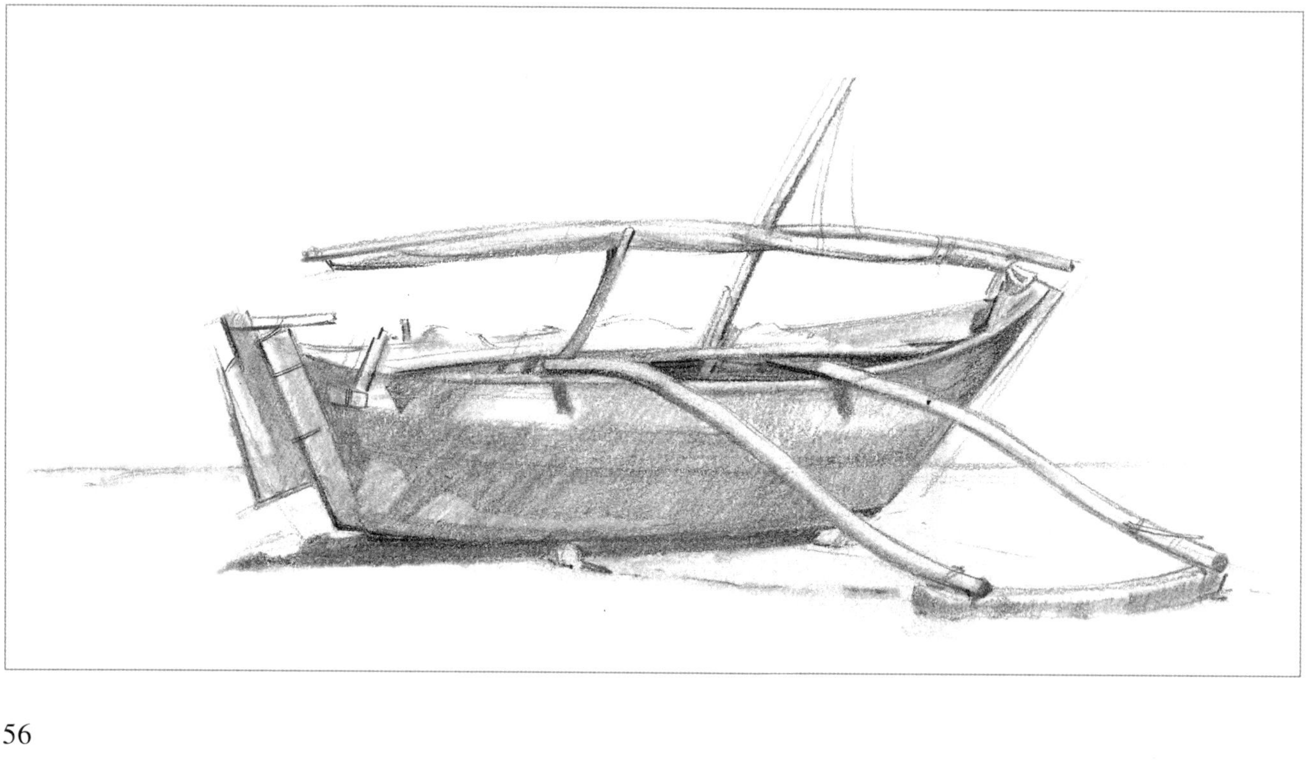

Cartridge Paper – 2B-4B

These are study sketches which have been done with focus on particular forms, their structure, shade-light effect etc. Such types of drawings on various subjects make good material for future references.

Drawing Paper- 2B

On both pages, these drawings are preliminary rough compositional sketches. These very small sketches (also called thumbnails) are mainly done for the purpose of determining composition, space division, and simplification of shade-light and consideration of tonal values.

A thumbnail is a part of an artist's creative process of developing painting. These are sometimes done using only lines, sometimes lines and tones, and at times using only the tonal values.

▲ *Bond Paper – 2B, 4B*

This drawing was composed by first using bold outline and clear forms, later adding smooth tones in some areas and textured tones in others.

Bond Paper – Graphite Stick 4B ▶

When a thin paper is placed on a surface with texture and a pencil rubbed over it, the texture of the surface is imprinted on the paper. This drawing has been done using similar technique on surfaces with different textures. Initial part of the drawing was to outline the form. Next, to achieve the texture of her straw hat, the surface of steel wire mesh window was used, for her hair, glass surface with vertical lines was used and for the dress, a surface with round circles design was used.

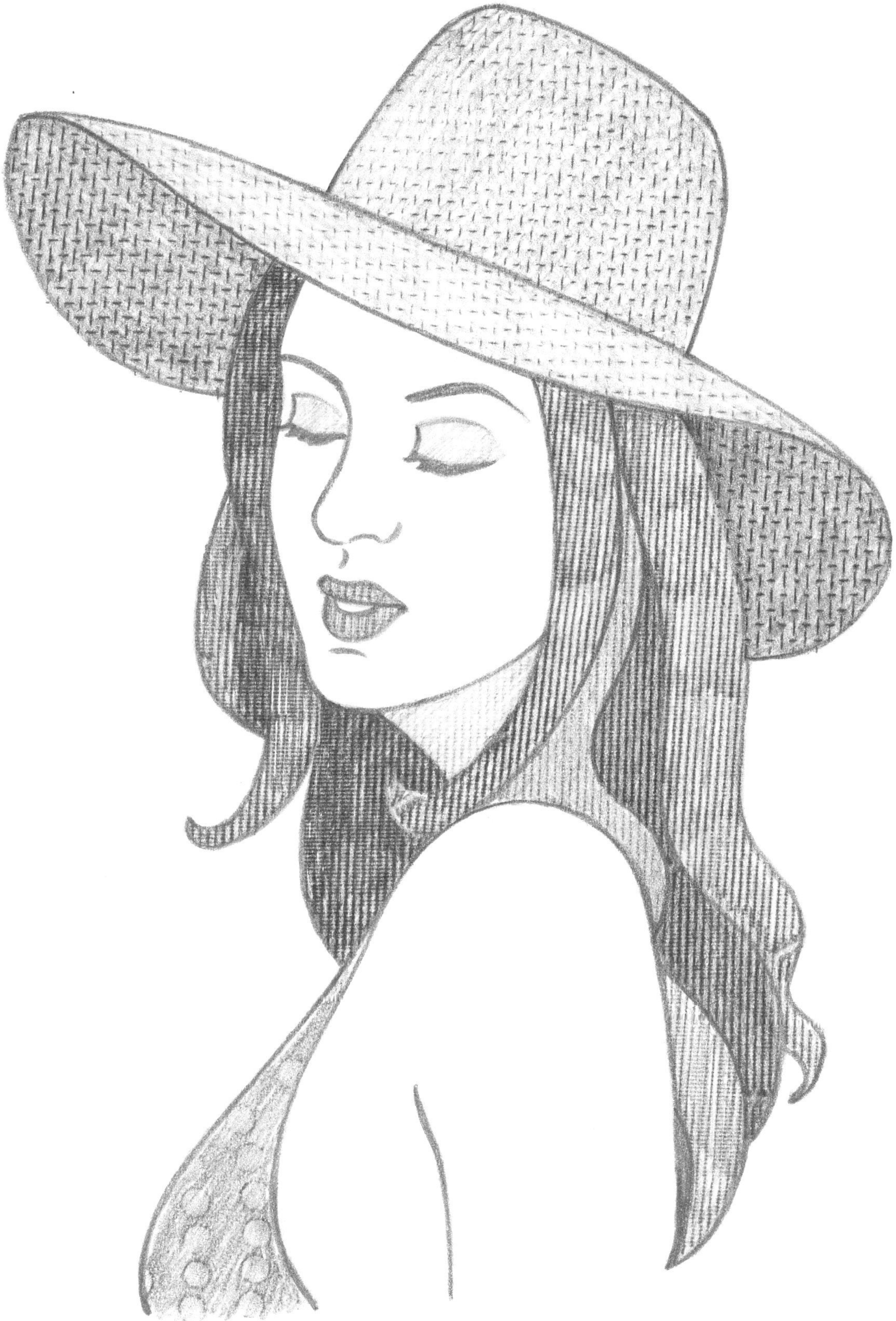

◀ *Drawing paper – Graphite Stick 4B*

To bring out the natural grace of this dancer, rhythmic lines with varying thicknesses have been used without showing any shade-light effect.

Super White cartridge – 6B ▶

In this drawing, the pencil was sharpened to a chisel point to get a bold thick line. To draw this person's hair and beard, slightly decorative elements were added to curved lines, which bring out the graceful beauty of these lines.

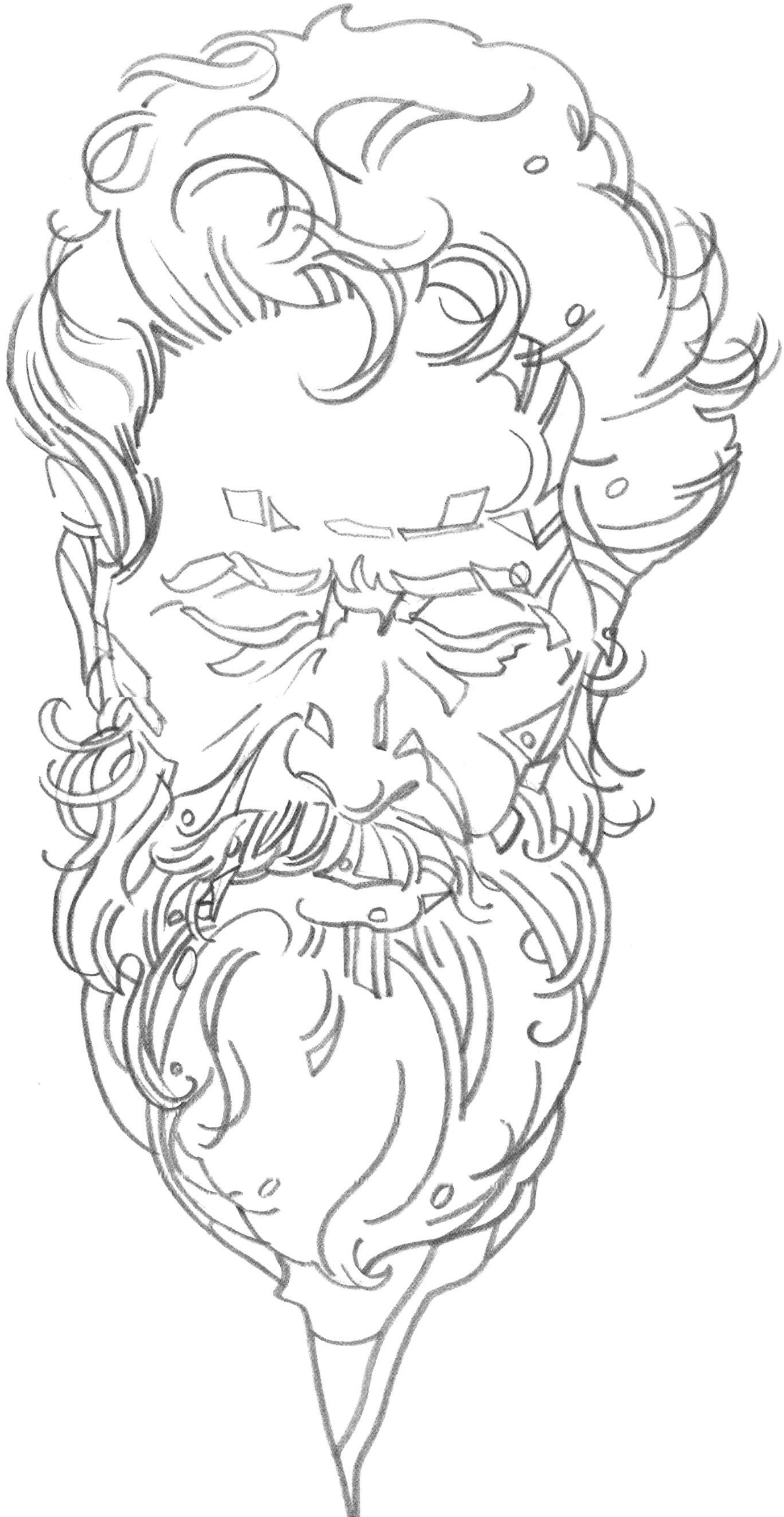

Square Block Textured Paper – 8B

We have already seen how to achieve different textures by rubbing pencil on textured papers on Page 8. Drawing done using such textures gives the picture a unique visual effect. Numerous experiments can be done similarly.

Drawing Paper – 6B

For tonal rendering of this bronze sculpture in Indian style, full tonal ranges of shade-light effect have been used. While observing the hard and soft edges, this drawing was finished by applying varying degrees of pressure on the pencil.

◀ *Drawing Paper – 4B*

This drawing is mainly a study of the folds that form on the clothing depending on the body structure. This was rendered by observing the body structure, shade-light and details of her clothes, and using suitable tones. Study of various types of draperies and their texture is an important part of art education.

Bond Paper – 2B, 4B ▶

The colourful costume of this tribal/Lamani woman is studded with tiny mirrors, beads and silver coins. When drawing such intricate forms, details of each individual area must be completed carefully while maintaining consistency of technique for the entire drawing.

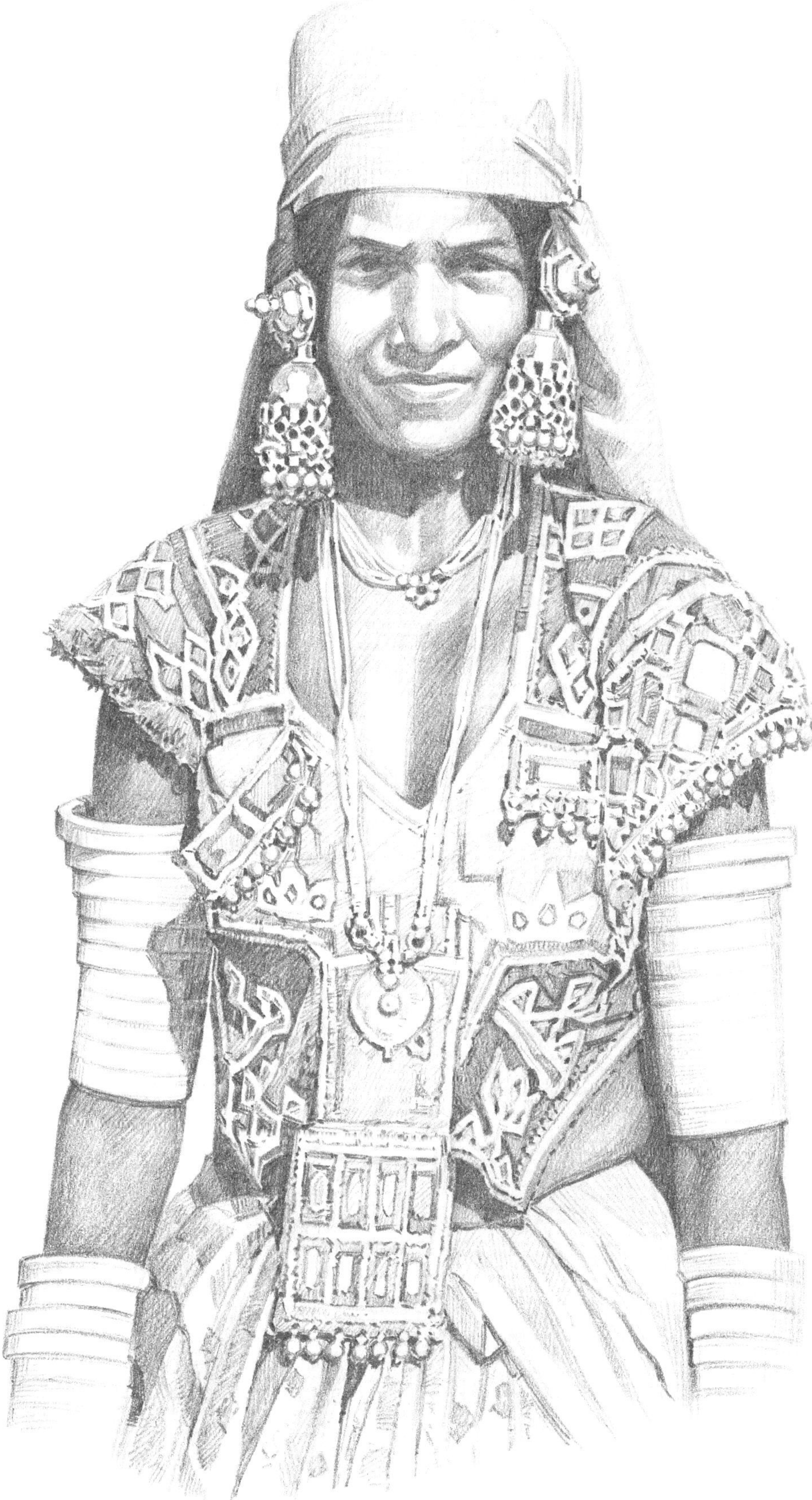

▲ *Drawing Paper – 6B*

This village scene was created during a sketching trip. To capture the environmental effect, full tonal range was used with a 6B pencil.

Drawing Paper – 2B-4B, Paper Stump ▶

After shading with pencil and then rubbed with a paper stump, a very soft effect is achieved. Similarly a paper stump is also used to evenly mix tones used in the drawing.

The foggy atmosphere of a winter morning and the reflections in the still water was effectively expressed by using this method. On the smooth texture obtained by paper stumps, linear marks and dark accents were used in some places completing the drawing.

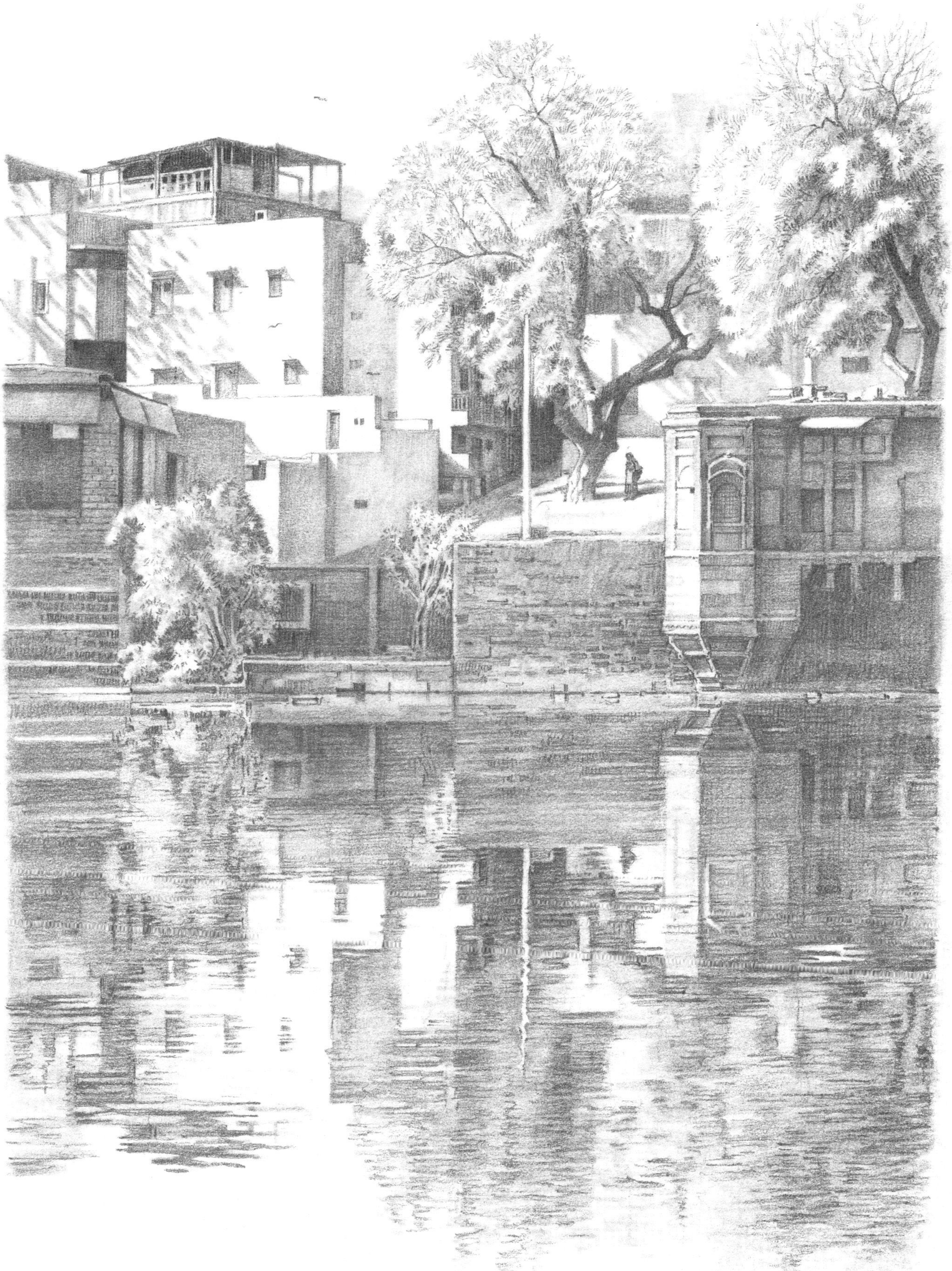

Bond Paper – H, 2H

This drawing was inspired by the pixelated image produced in a computer. In a digital image, countless tiny squares called pixels come together forming a complete picture. To achieve this effect, small squares were outlined at a distance of 1/16 inches each and then tone was added gradually to each square defining the form. This technique has given a unique visual quality to a realistic subject.

71

Super White Cartridge – 6B

The pencil point was whittled away to make it slanting like a quill and resembling a chisel point. The chisel point is useful to quickly fill up even tones and it gives small and longer strokes of same thickness. Also, using the point fine lines can be achieved. The drawing above is done using this technique to express the mountain peaks, craggy topography of the mountains and the shade-light effect on them, giving a unique personality to the picture.

Super White Cartridge – 8B

This scene is a crowded street in Jaisalmer, showing buildings and shops laden with various merchandise lining the street from both sides, and crowds of people making their way through all this. Such a subject is complex and normally contains many components at the same time, but while drawing, it is important to simplify the subjects in a suggestive manner. The essence of such a subject can be captured effectively well by this process.

▲ *Drawing Paper – Carpenter Pencil*

While using a flat pencil such as a carpenter pencil, its flat side can be used for side strokes and its edge for straight lines. Due to the bold strokes of the pencil, shade-light effect is automatically simplified, yet there are limitations on the darkness of tones obtained by this pencil.

Super White Cartridge – 8B ▶

An 8B pencil is very soft and by applying varying degrees of pressure, we can easily get light to very dark tones. Above drawing was made using this very quality of 8B pencil.

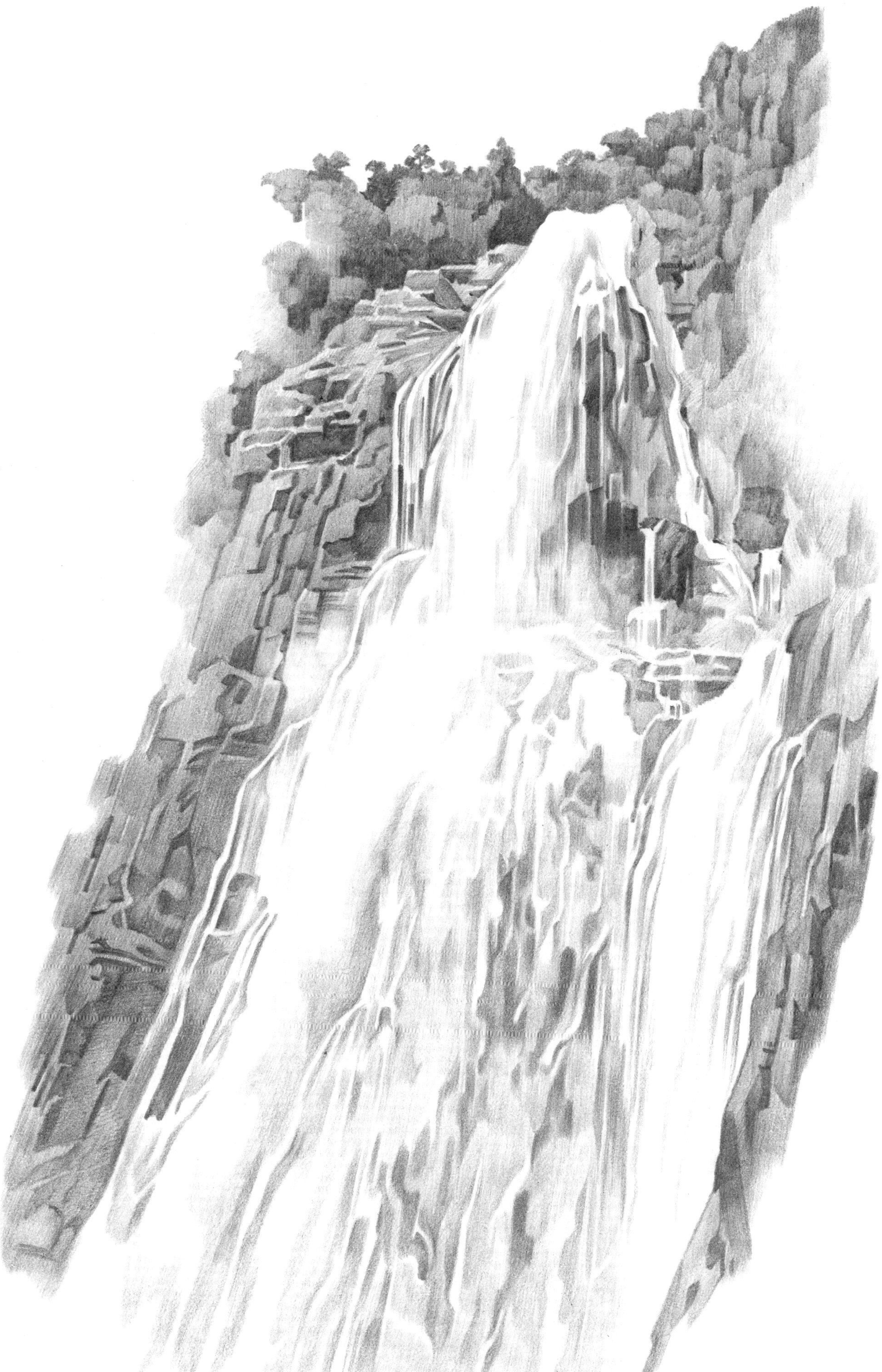

▲ *Super White Cartridge – 2B*

Free hatching technique is used for this drawing. The direction of the hatching follows the moulding of the form, using cross hatching for darker tones.

Super White Cartridge – H, HB ▶

Members of a shepherd family, their lifestyle and associated elements have been portrayed in this composition. For this, creative freedom is taken to produce a montage of various forms and elements. To show their rough and tough lifestyle which is close to nature, free hatching and cross hatching technique is employed. This type of composition is useful in various forms of illustrations.

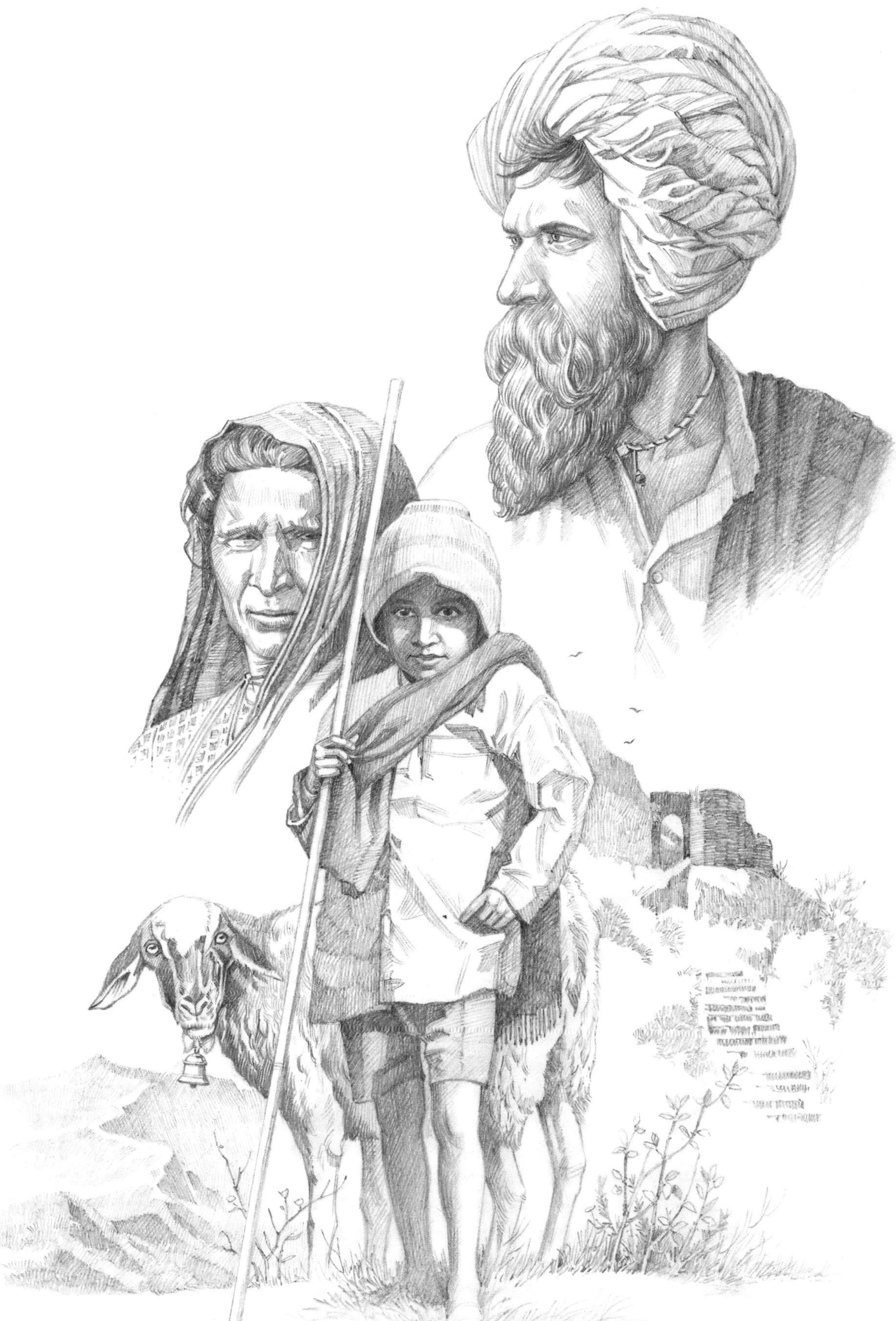

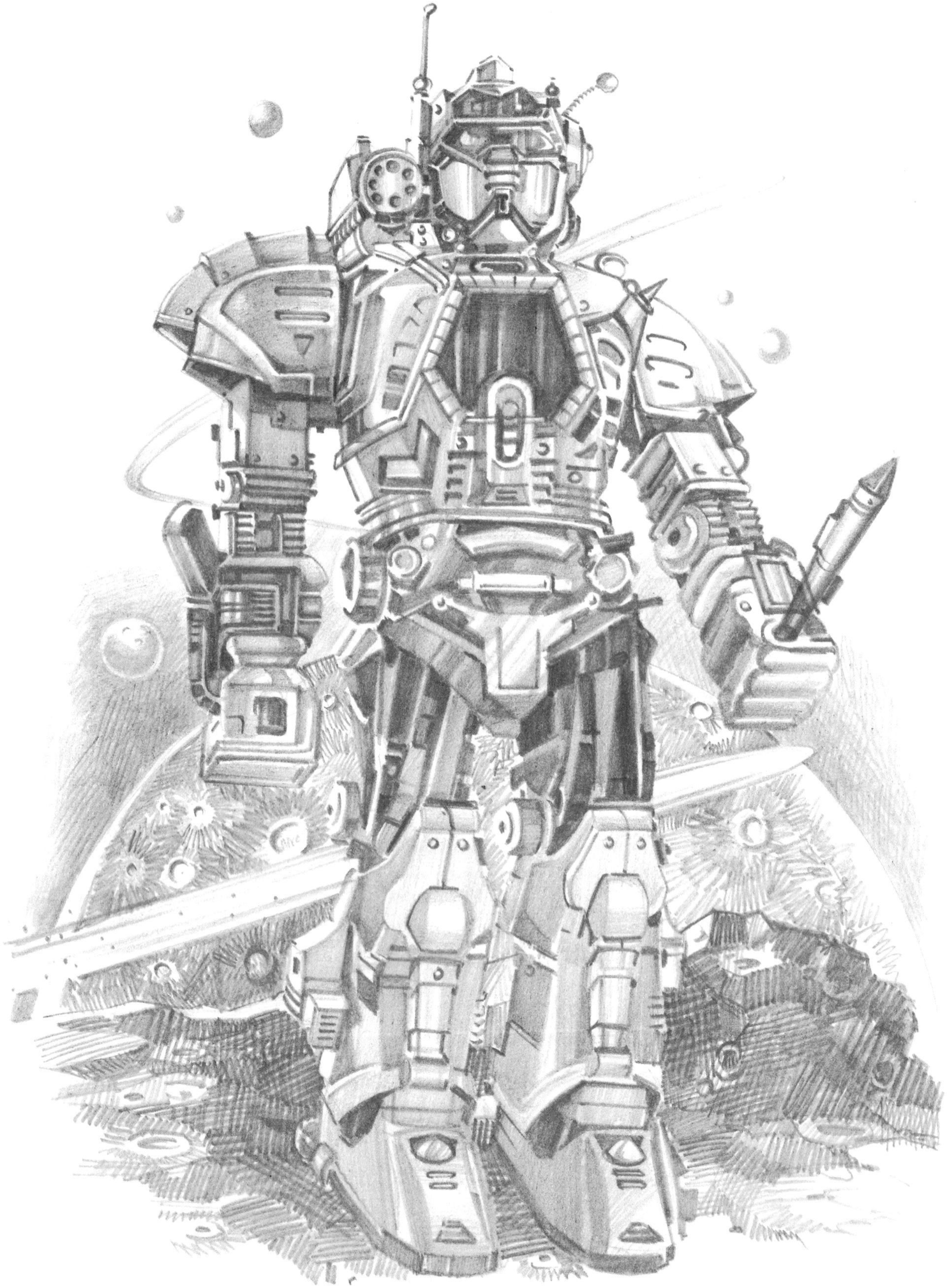